JOSH STEVE

Currency Conspiracy

Copyright © 2023 by Josh Steve

All rights reserved. No part of this publication may be reproduced, stored or transmitted in any form or by any means, electronic, mechanical, photocopying, recording, scanning, or otherwise without written permission from the publisher. It is illegal to copy this book, post it to a website, or distribute it by any other means without permission.

This novel is entirely a work of fiction. The names, characters and incidents portrayed in it are the work of the author's imagination. Any resemblance to actual persons, living or dead, events or localities is entirely coincidental.

Josh Steve asserts the moral right to be identified as the author of this work.

First edition

This book was professionally typeset on Reedsy.
Find out more at reedsy.com

Contents

The Mysterious Insider	1
Unexplained Disappearances	5
Clues in the Code	9
The Cryptic Message	12
The Underground Trading Ring	16
A Race Against Time	21
The Tangled Web	25
The Unraveling	30
A Dangerous Gamble	35
The Unveiling	40
Infiltration	45
A Dangerous Revelation	50

The Mysterious Insider

Detective Mark Turner had seen his fair share of wild swings in the forex market. As a seasoned investigator specializing in financial crimes, he'd navigated the treacherous waters of insider trading, market manipulation, and white-collar criminals. But what he stumbled upon that fateful Thursday evening was unlike anything he'd encountered before.

It was a rainy night in Manhattan, the kind of night that washed the city in shades of silver and made the neon lights of Wall Street glisten with an eerie allure. Mark stood on a dimly lit street corner, the collar of his trench coat turned up against the drizzle. He was waiting for his contact, a whistleblower who claimed to have information about a massive currency conspiracy.

His breath formed misty clouds in the cold air as he watched the city's hustle and bustle continue unabated. People hurried past him, clutching umbrellas and briefcases, oblivious to the financial storm that was brewing behind closed doors.

Suddenly, a figure emerged from the shadows, moving with the fluid grace of a panther. Mark's pulse quickened as the man approached. He was tall and wiry, his face hidden beneath the hood of a soaked black hoodie.

"Detective Turner?" the man's voice was a whisper, barely audible above the rain's gentle drumming on the pavement.

Mark nodded, keeping his eyes locked on the mysterious informant. "That's me. You have information about the currency conspiracy?"

The informant didn't reply immediately. Instead, he glanced around nervously before leading Mark into a narrow alleyway, away from prying eyes. The air grew heavy with anticipation as they entered the shadows.

"I can't reveal my identity," the informant said, his voice hushed. "But I've seen things, things that should never have happened in the forex market."

Mark leaned in, his instincts as sharp as ever. "Start from the beginning. Tell me everything."

The informant took a deep breath, his hood falling back to reveal a gaunt, worried face. "It all started six months ago. I work for a major brokerage firm, one of the big players in the forex market. At first, it seemed like a series of unusual trading patterns, but then it became clear that someone was manipulating the market."

Mark listened intently, his mind racing. Market manipulation was nothing new, but the scale of this operation seemed unprecedented.

"They call him 'The Insider,'" the informant continued. "No one knows who he is, but he's been making billions by controlling currency prices. He's unstoppable, and everyone who tries to expose him disappears."

Mark's curiosity turned to concern. "Disappears? What do you mean?"

The informant's eyes darted around once more, as if he expected shadows to come to life. "People who get too close to the truth vanish, Mark. Traders, analysts, even investigators like you. I've seen it happen. I've seen careers ruined, lives destroyed."

Mark could feel the weight of the informant's words settling over him. This was no ordinary case; it was a web of intrigue and danger that reached deep into the heart of the financial world.

"Can you provide any evidence?" Mark asked, his voice low.

The informant reached into the inner pocket of his hoodie and produced a small flash drive. He handed it to Mark with trembling hands. "This contains documents, transactions, and communications that expose The Insider's operation. I've risked everything to get this to you."

Mark took the flash drive, his heart pounding with a mixture of excitement and dread. "Thank you," he said sincerely. "You've done the right thing."

Just as Mark was about to ask another question, a sudden noise echoed through the alley. Footsteps. He turned, but it was too late. A group of shadowy figures emerged from the darkness, surrounding them.

The informant's face turned ashen, and he whispered, "They found us."

Mark's adrenaline surged as he assessed the situation. These were no ordinary thugs; they were professionals. His hand went instinctively to the holster under his coat, but before he could draw his weapon, a powerful blow struck him from behind. Pain exploded in his head, and the world spun.

As Mark crumpled to the ground, losing consciousness, he saw the informant being dragged away by the assailants. The last thing he heard was a cold, mocking voice saying, "Looks like The Insider sent his regards, Detective."

And then darkness consumed him, leaving him with a burning determination to unravel the enigma of The Insider and rescue the informant who had risked it all to expose the currency conspiracy.

Unexplained Disappearances

Pain surged through Mark Turner's head like a relentless tide as consciousness returned. He groaned, his vision blurry, and his senses slowly sharpening. Blinking away the haze, he realized he was lying on a cold, damp concrete floor in a dimly lit room.

As the throbbing in his head began to ebb, Mark took stock of his surroundings. The room was small, with walls made of rough, gray bricks, and a single bare lightbulb dangled from the ceiling, casting harsh shadows. The air was thick with the musty scent of dampness, and the sound of distant dripping water was a constant reminder of his predicament.

Struggling to sit up, Mark's hand instinctively went to his side, where his holster should have been. It was empty. They'd taken his weapon, leaving him vulnerable in this unknown place.

A wave of panic threatened to consume him, but he fought it down. He needed to focus. He needed to find out where he was, who had captured him, and what had happened to the informant.

Pushing himself to his feet, Mark staggered toward the door, his footsteps echoing ominously in the confined space. He gripped the cold, metal handle and cautiously turned it. The door creaked open, revealing a narrow corridor bathed in the same dim light.

Mark hesitated for a moment, his senses on high alert. He had no idea who his captors were or what they wanted. But he couldn't stay trapped in this room. Taking a deep breath, he stepped out into the corridor, his every nerve tingling with anticipation.

The corridor led to a branching network of dimly lit passages, each one seemingly identical to the last. Mark moved cautiously, trying to keep track of his route, but it was an impossible maze. Panic threatened to take hold again as he realized the gravity of his situation. He was lost in this underground labyrinth.

As he turned a corner, Mark heard voices, hushed but distinct. He pressed himself against the cold wall and strained to listen. It was a conversation in low tones, and he recognized one of the voices—it belonged to the informant.

"...no, I won't tell you anything else," the informant's voice was resolute, filled with determination.

Another voice, colder and more menacing, replied, "You're in no position to refuse, my friend. You've seen too much."

Mark's heart raced. He had to get to the informant, to rescue him, and retrieve the valuable evidence they had risked their life to provide. Carefully, he continued down the corridor toward the source of the voices.

Around another corner, he finally spotted them. The informant was bound to a rusty chair, his face bruised and battered but still defiant. Standing over him was a tall man in a sharp suit, his face obscured by shadows.

Mark needed a plan. He glanced around the corridor, searching for any makeshift weapon. His eyes fell on a length of rusty pipe discarded in a corner. It wasn't much, but it would have to do.

He picked it up and edged closer, his steps as silent as a cat stalking its prey. The corridor was narrow, and the shadows played in his favor. He gripped the pipe tightly, ready to strike.

But just as he was about to launch his rescue, the informant's defiant voice stopped him cold. "You may have captured me, but you'll never break me. The truth will come out."

The man in the suit chuckled, a sound devoid of humor. "We'll see about that, my friend. The Insider has ways of dealing with those who pose a threat."

The Insider. Mark's heart raced. This was a direct connection to the enigmatic manipulator of the forex market, the one responsible for the chaos in the financial world. He couldn't let them break the informant.

With renewed determination, Mark lunged forward, swinging the rusty pipe with all his strength. The makeshift weapon struck the suit-clad man's hand, causing him to cry out in pain as he dropped a menacing-looking device.

Chaos erupted as Mark fought to free the informant. They struggled against their captors, punches landing, and adrenaline surging. Mark's mind was a whirlwind of fear, anger, and resolve.

Finally, with a well-placed kick, Mark sent one of the captors sprawling backward, creating enough space to free the informant. They scrambled to their feet, and together, they overpowered the remaining captors.

The informant retrieved the device the suit-clad man had dropped, his hands trembling. "This... this is what they were going to use to break me. It's a truth serum, Mark. They wanted to force me to reveal everything I knew about The Insider."

Mark's eyes narrowed. "We need to get out of here, and fast. But before we go, we need to find out who these people are working for, who's behind The Insider."

The informant nodded and handed Mark the device, which he pocketed. They moved swiftly through the maze of corridors, retracing Mark's steps until they reached the room where he had first awakened.

With the informant's help, Mark forced open a window, revealing a dimly lit alley below. They climbed through and staggered out into the cold night, leaving behind the underground labyrinth.

As they made their escape, Mark couldn't help but wonder how deep the conspiracy went, and what kind of power The Insider wielded to make people vanish. The battle against this mysterious figure was far from over, and Mark was more determined than ever to uncover the truth and bring those responsible to justice.

Clues in the Code

The early morning sun cast long shadows across the city as Detective Mark Turner and the informant, whose real name was David, found refuge in a small, nondescript apartment. It was a temporary safe haven where they could regroup and assess the evidence David had risked his life to provide.

Mark watched as David paced the room, his agitation evident. The walls of the apartment were painted a fading beige, and the furnishings were minimal, making the space feel stark and impersonal. The silence between them was heavy, pregnant with unspoken questions.

Finally, David broke the silence. "Mark, you need to understand how deep this goes. The Insider's network is vast, and I've only scratched the surface. The evidence I gave you is just the tip of the iceberg."

Mark nodded, his gaze fixed on the flash drive containing the incriminating evidence. "I know, David. But this is a start. We can use it to unravel the conspiracy, to expose The Insider and those who protect him."

David took a deep breath, his fingers trembling as he reached for a laptop on a small wooden table. "I can help you analyze the data, Mark. I've been gathering information for months, but I'm not a hacker. I don't have the skills to dig deeper into The Insider's digital footprint."

Mark appreciated David's dedication, but he also knew the risks involved. "It's dangerous, David. The Insider's people will be looking for us. Are you sure you want to get involved even further?"

David's eyes held a steely determination. "I've come this far, Mark. I can't back down now. I need to see this through, for the sake of all those who've suffered because of The Insider's actions."

Mark nodded in agreement. There was no turning back now. He connected the flash drive to the laptop, and David's fingers flew across the keyboard as he accessed the encrypted files. Lines of code and financial data filled the screen, an intricate puzzle that held the secrets of The Insider's operations.

As David delved into the data, Mark's mind raced. The Insider had manipulated the forex market on a massive scale, causing financial turmoil worldwide. But why? What was the ultimate goal? And who was The Insider's mysterious benefactor?

Hours passed as David and Mark worked tirelessly, deciphering the complex algorithms and sifting through countless financial transactions. They discovered patterns, anomalies, and hidden messages within the code, but the true extent of The Insider's plan remained elusive.

Then, as the sun dipped below the horizon, David's eyes widened in realization. "Mark, look at this," he said, pointing to a section of code on the screen.

Mark leaned closer, his heart pounding with anticipation. It was a series of complex calculations, but within them was a hidden message, written in a code only a seasoned forex trader could decipher. It read, "The Insider's plan: Destabilize economies, seize power, change the world."

Mark's mind reeled. The Insider's motives were becoming clearer, but the scope of their ambition was staggering. They weren't just out for financial gain; they aimed to reshape the global order itself.

"We need to find out who The Insider is and who's pulling their strings," Mark said, his voice filled with resolve.

David nodded, his eyes burning with determination. "I've managed to trace some of the transactions back to a shell company, but it's just a front. We need to dig deeper, find the real identity of The Insider."

The duo worked through the night, tracking down leads, uncovering hidden financial connections, and piecing together a puzzle that extended far beyond the forex market. The Insider's network spanned across borders, involving powerful individuals and organizations with their own agendas.

As dawn broke, Mark and David were exhausted but driven by a shared sense of purpose. They knew they were getting closer to the truth, but they were also aware that their pursuit of The Insider had made them targets.

Mark glanced at his watch. "We can't stay here any longer. We need to move, stay one step ahead of them. Let's pack up what we have and find a more secure location."

David nodded, and they carefully disconnected the laptop, ensuring that no trace of their activities remained behind. As they left the apartment, Mark couldn't shake the feeling that they were racing against time, that the forces aligned with The Insider were closing in on them.

The next chapter of their investigation would take them deeper into the heart of the conspiracy, bringing them face to face with powerful adversaries and unveiling shocking revelations that would challenge everything they thought they knew about The Insider and the currency conspiracy that threatened to change the world.

The Cryptic Message

The moon hung low in the night sky, casting a silvery glow over the city as Detective Mark Turner and David, the informant, huddled in a dimly lit, nondescript motel room. They had been on the run for days, moving from one safe haven to another, always one step ahead of those who sought to silence them.

David sat at a worn-out wooden table, the glow of his laptop screen casting eerie shadows across his face. He had become an adept hacker, tracing financial transactions and unearthing hidden connections with the skill of a seasoned investigator.

Mark stood by the motel room window, peering out through the gap in the moth-eaten curtains. The street below was deserted, the city shrouded in a blanket of silence. It was the calm before the storm, and Mark couldn't shake the feeling that their every move was being watched.

"We're getting closer," David said, breaking the tense silence. "I've managed to trace some of The Insider's transactions to a series of offshore accounts. It's a convoluted web, but I think we can unravel it."

Mark turned away from the window and approached David, his senses on high alert. "What have you found?"

David's fingers danced across the keyboard as he brought up a list of encrypted messages that had been exchanged between The Insider and their collaborators. "There's a pattern to these messages, Mark. They're coded, but I've been working on deciphering them."

Mark leaned in closer, studying the screen. The messages were a mix of numbers, symbols, and seemingly random characters. "Have you made any progress?"

David nodded. "I've managed to crack a few of the messages. They contain instructions, details about currency movements, and even mentions of specific individuals who are part of this conspiracy."

Mark's heart quickened. They were on the brink of a breakthrough. "What else have you discovered?"

David hesitated for a moment, his gaze fixed on the screen. "There's one message, Mark, that stands out. It's different from the rest. It's not just about financial transactions; it's something more… ominous."

Mark felt a chill run down his spine. "Show me."

David clicked on the message, and the screen displayed a series of characters that looked like gibberish at first glance. But as Mark studied them, he realized that there was a method to the madness. It was a code, and it contained a message hidden within.

The message read: "The Insider's plan is more than just money. It's about power and control. The world will change, and those who oppose will vanish."

Mark's jaw clenched. The Insider's motives were becoming clearer, but the cryptic message hinted at something far more sinister. They weren't just manipulating currency markets; they were orchestrating a global shift in power.

"We need to find out who's receiving these messages," Mark said, his voice taut with determination.

David nodded. "I've been tracking the IP addresses and digital footprints of the recipients. They all lead to a central server, but it's heavily encrypted. Breaking through will take time."

Time was a luxury they couldn't afford. Mark knew that with every passing moment, The Insider's plan inched closer to fruition. "We need to act fast, David. The longer this conspiracy remains hidden, the harder it will be to stop."

David's fingers flew across the keyboard as he initiated a series of hacking tools to breach the server's defenses. Mark paced the room, his thoughts racing. They needed a lead, someone on the inside who could help them uncover The Insider's identity and the full scope of their plan.

Just as Mark was about to suggest reaching out to one of their contacts in the financial world, David let out a triumphant exclamation. "I've got it! I've breached the server. We can access the recipient list and see who's been receiving these messages."

Mark leaned over David's shoulder, his heart pounding. The screen displayed a list of names, some of them familiar figures in the world of finance and politics. But one name stood out, a name that sent a shiver down Mark's spine.

Adrian Masters.

Adrian Masters was a powerful billionaire with deep ties to international politics and finance. He had always operated in the shadows, manipulating events from behind the scenes. If he was involved with The Insider, it meant that this conspiracy reached the highest echelons of power.

"We need to confront Adrian Masters," Mark said, his voice low and determined. "He might be the key to unraveling The Insider's plan and exposing the truth."

David nodded, his eyes filled with a mix of determination and fear. 'But Mark, confronting someone like Masters is dangerous. He has resources, connections, and a ruthless reputation."

Mark knew the risks, but he also knew that there was no turning back now. They had come too far, uncovered too much, to stop. The only path forward was to confront Adrian Masters and force him to reveal The Insider's true identity and the extent of their plan.

As they prepared to leave the motel room, Mark couldn't shake the feeling that they were walking into a web of danger and deception from which there might be no escape. But he was committed to the pursuit of justice, no matter the cost, and he would stop at nothing to expose The Insider's currency conspiracy and protect the world from its dire consequences.

The Underground Trading Ring

The night was a shroud of darkness as Detective Mark Turner and David, the informant, drove through the rain-soaked streets of the city. Their destination was a high-end nightclub rumored to be a front for one of Adrian Masters' illicit operations. Mark couldn't shake the feeling that confronting Masters was their best chance to uncover the identity of The Insider and expose the currency conspiracy.

The nightclub's neon sign flickered in the rain, casting an eerie glow on the wet pavement. Mark and David parked a block away to avoid drawing attention. The club's entrance was guarded by two imposing bouncers who eyed the approaching duo with suspicion.

David leaned in close to Mark, his voice barely above a whisper. "Remember, Mark, we're going in undercover. We don't want to tip off Masters or The Insider's associates."

Mark nodded, his pulse quickening with anticipation. They had assumed false identities, posing as traders looking to make a deal within the secretive world of high-stakes currency trading. It was a dangerous game, but the only way to get close to Masters and the heart of the conspiracy.

As they approached the entrance, Mark kept his gaze straight ahead, avoiding eye contact with the bouncers. David, with his charm and charisma, took the lead, engaging the bouncers in conversation about forex trading strategies and the allure of the nightclub.

The bouncers exchanged glances but eventually waved them through. Mark and David stepped into a world of dimly lit opulence. The nightclub's interior was a tapestry of plush velvet, gold accents, and low-hanging chandeliers. The air was thick with the scent of expensive perfumes and the rhythmic thump of electronic music.

They made their way to the bar, where the clientele consisted of impeccably dressed traders, financiers, and a few shadowy figures lurking in the corners. Mark couldn't help but feel like a small fish in a vast, treacherous sea.

David signaled to the bartender and ordered two drinks. Mark's gaze darted around the room, searching for any sign of Adrian Masters or a connection to The Insider. But the place was a maze of noise and distraction, making it nearly impossible to eavesdrop on conversations or spot their target.

Their drinks arrived, and David handed one to Mark. "Keep your eyes peeled, Mark. Masters might not be here himself, but his associates are likely to show up."

Mark nodded and took a sip of his drink, his senses on high alert. He watched as traders exchanged hushed conversations, their gestures conveying secrets that could shake the financial world. It was a world of illusion, where fortunes were made and lost with a click of a button.

As the night wore on, David engaged in conversation with a group of traders, subtly probing for information about the nightclub's connections. Mark continued to scan the room, searching for any familiar faces or clues that would lead them to Masters or The Insider.

Then, as the music throbbed and the night grew darker, Mark spotted something—a discreet hand signal exchanged between two traders at a corner table. It was a signal he had seen before, one that indicated a covert transaction was taking place.

He tapped David on the shoulder and discreetly pointed to the traders. David nodded and excused himself from his conversation, joining Mark as they moved closer to the corner table.

The traders, a man and a woman, were engrossed in their conversation, oblivious to Mark and David's approach. Mark strained to listen, catching snippets of their discussion.

"…profits are soaring… thanks to The Insider…"

Mark's heart raced. The mention of The Insider confirmed that they were on the right track. But the traders' conversation was guarded, and they spoke in code, making it difficult to decipher their exact connection to The Insider.

Just as Mark was about to make a move, a voice cut through the air like a cold blade. "Gentlemen, enjoying the evening?"

They turned to see a tall, well-dressed man approaching, his eyes sharp and calculating. It was Adrian Masters.

David remained composed, offering a polite smile. "Mr. Masters, what a pleasant surprise. We were just discussing the intricacies of forex trading."

Masters' gaze lingered on them, his smile a thin, enigmatic line. "Forex trading, you say? How fascinating. But this isn't the place for business discussions. Perhaps we can continue our conversation in private?"

Mark's heart pounded. This was their chance to get closer to Masters, to uncover the truth. He nodded in agreement, and they followed Masters through a discreet doorway at the back of the nightclub.

The room they entered was a stark contrast to the vibrant chaos outside. It was a quiet, dimly lit chamber, furnished with leather couches and a mahogany table. Masters gestured for them to sit.

Once they were seated, Masters fixed his sharp gaze on them. "I must admit, I'm intrigued by your interest in forex trading. But I have a keen eye for talent, and I sense that you're not here simply for profit. What is it you're really after?"

Mark exchanged a glance with David, knowing that their true identities were at stake. But they couldn't afford to back down now. David spoke carefully, choosing his words with precision. "Mr. Masters, we've heard whispers about an organization, one that wields significant power in the forex market. We wish to become part of that world, to contribute to its success."

Masters leaned back in his chair, his expression unreadable. "You have ambition, I'll give you that. But this world isn't for the faint of heart. It requires dedication, loyalty, and discretion."

Mark nodded, playing along. "We understand the stakes, Mr. Masters. We're willing to prove our dedication."

Masters' eyes gleamed with a calculating glint. "Very well. There is a test, a trial of sorts, for those who seek to enter this world. Complete it successfully, and you may find yourselves on the inside."

Mark and David exchanged a knowing look. This was their chance to gain access to The Insider's operation, to get closer to the heart of the conspiracy. They nodded in agreement.

Masters leaned in, his voice low and conspiratorial. "I'll provide you with a set of coordinates. There, you'll find an underground trading ring. Complete the challenge they present to you, and you'll have taken your first step into our world."

As Masters handed them a piece of paper with the coordinates, Mark couldn't help but wonder what awaited them in the underground trading ring. It was a test, a trial of their loyalty and determination, but it was also a perilous journey into the heart of The Insider's conspiracy.

They left the dim chamber, their minds racing with questions and uncertainty. But one thing was clear—they were getting closer to The Insider, closer to exposing the currency conspiracy that threatened to change the world. The path ahead was treacherous, but they were committed to seeing it through, no matter the cost.

A Race Against Time

The coordinates provided by Adrian Masters led Mark Turner and David to a desolate industrial district on the outskirts of the city. It was the dead of night, and the only sound that pierced the silence was the distant hum of machinery from the abandoned factories that loomed like dark giants against the moonless sky.

The address they had received led them to a nondescript building, its windows shattered, and its exterior covered in graffiti. The place exuded an eerie, abandoned atmosphere that sent shivers down Mark's spine.

Mark and David parked their car a short distance away, opting for a cautious approach. They knew that whatever awaited them inside could be a test of their loyalty or a trap set by The Insider's network.

"We should be prepared for anything," Mark cautioned as they donned black clothing and concealed their weapons. The stakes had never been higher, and they couldn't afford any mistakes.

David nodded, his expression resolute. "Agreed. Let's stick together, watch each other's backs."

With their plan in place, they approached the building, moving like shadows in the night. The entrance was a rusted steel door covered in graffiti, a stark contrast to the opulent world they had encountered at the nightclub.

Mark cautiously tried the door, and to his surprise, it creaked open with minimal resistance. The darkness inside was oppressive, swallowing the feeble light from their flashlights as they ventured further into the unknown.

As they explored the labyrinthine corridors of the building, a sense of foreboding settled over them. It was as though the walls themselves held secrets, and the silence was pregnant with anticipation.

They descended a narrow staircase into an underground chamber that resembled an old storage area. The air was stale, and the room was dimly lit by flickering fluorescent lights. In the center of the chamber, they spotted a group of individuals huddled together, their faces obscured by masks and shadows.

One of the masked figures stepped forward, a sinister grin curling beneath the fabric of the mask. "Welcome, newcomers. You've come seeking entrance to our world, have you not?"

Mark and David exchanged a wary glance before David replied, "Yes, we're here to prove ourselves. What's the challenge?"

The masked figure pointed to a table in the corner of the chamber. On it lay a pile of currency notes, foreign and domestic, in various denominations. "You have one hour to turn these notes into a profit. Use whatever means necessary, but remember, only the successful shall be welcomed."

Mark and David approached the table, their eyes scanning the currency notes. It was a daunting challenge, and they knew that time was not on their side. They had to think fast, strategize, and make the right decisions to succeed.

David began sorting through the notes, his mind racing as he considered potential trading strategies. Mark, on the other hand, started making inquiries among the masked figures, trying to gather information about the underground trading ring and its connections to The Insider.

The masked individuals were tight-lipped, offering cryptic responses that hinted at a deeper, more complex network. They spoke in riddles, revealing little but suggesting that success in this challenge would earn them entry into a world of immense power and influence.

As the minutes ticked away, Mark and David's desperation grew. The currency notes were a puzzle, a financial Rubik's Cube that seemed impossible to solve. The masked figures watched them with cold, unyielding eyes, their silence a constant reminder of the stakes involved.

Then, with only minutes to spare, David had a breakthrough. He identified a fluctuation in the exchange rate of a particular currency pair and executed a series of rapid trades using the notes on the table. With each successful trade, their profit margin increased.

Mark, meanwhile, had managed to glean a few vital pieces of information from the masked figures. They spoke of a mysterious figure known as "The Collector," a person who controlled this underground trading ring and was rumored to be closely tied to The Insider.

With their hour nearly gone, David executed one final trade, and the room fell into a tense silence. The masked figures watched as the numbers on the screen displayed a substantial profit.

The masked figure who had issued the challenge stepped forward once more, his expression inscrutable. "Impressive. You've passed our test. You may leave this place and consider yourselves initiated."

Mark and David exchanged a relieved look, but their victory was tempered by the knowledge that they had entered a world shrouded in secrecy and danger. They couldn't let their guard down for a moment, not when The Collector and The Insider were still at large.

As they left the underground trading ring behind, Mark couldn't help but wonder about the connection between the challenge they had faced and The Insider's larger plan. What role did this secretive world of currency trading play in the grand scheme of the conspiracy?

Their journey had taken them deeper into the heart of darkness, and the race against time had only intensified. The pursuit of The Insider and the exposure of the currency conspiracy were more perilous than ever, and Mark knew that every step brought them closer to the truth, but also closer to the shadows that threatened to engulf them.

The Tangled Web

The night had grown colder as Detective Mark Turner and David, the informant, made their way back to their car parked on the desolate streets of the industrial district. The challenge set by the underground trading ring had granted them entry, but it had also left them with more questions than answers.

Mark gripped the steering wheel, his thoughts a whirlwind of uncertainty. "We gained access, but we're still in the dark about The Insider's true identity and the extent of their plan. What's the next move, David?"

David leaned back in his seat, his expression troubled. "We need to keep digging, Mark. The Collector and this underground trading ring are just pieces of the puzzle. We're getting closer, but there's more to uncover."

Mark nodded, his resolve unwavering. "Agreed. Let's regroup and analyze the information we've gathered so far. We'll figure out our next steps from there."

They drove back to their temporary safehouse, a secluded cabin in the woods, far away from prying eyes. The cabin was dimly lit, and a fire crackled in the stone fireplace, casting dancing shadows across the room.

David connected his laptop to the cabin's Wi-Fi, and Mark retrieved the flash drive containing the evidence they had gathered. Together, they began to piece together the puzzle of The Insider's conspiracy.

Hours turned into the early morning as they sifted through the data, connecting dots and identifying patterns. The evidence pointed to The Collector as a key figure in The Insider's operation, but the true identity of The Collector remained elusive.

David leaned forward, his fingers flying across the keyboard. "I've managed to trace some of The Collector's digital footprints to a server in Switzerland. It's heavily encrypted, but I believe it holds the answers we're looking for."

Mark's eyes narrowed. Switzerland was known for its secretive banking laws and safe havens for illicit operations. It made sense that The Collector would have ties to such a place. "Can you breach the server?"

David hesitated for a moment before nodding. "I believe so, but it won't be easy. The encryption is formidable, and The Collector's network is well-protected."

Mark knew they were risking everything by attempting to access the server, but there was no turning back now. The pursuit of justice and the exposure of The Insider's conspiracy demanded it. "Let's do it. We can't afford to wait any longer."

David initiated a series of hacking tools, his focus unwavering as he navigated through layers of encryption. Mark watched in tense anticipation, knowing that every second counted.

Finally, after what felt like an eternity, David's face lit up with triumph. "I've breached it, Mark. We're in."

The screen displayed a vast array of encrypted files, each one a potential key to unlocking the secrets of The Collector and The Insider. Mark and David began to sift through the data, their excitement tempered by the gravity of their discovery.

Among the files, they uncovered a series of encrypted emails that shed light on The Collector's network. The emails referenced a "master plan" and hinted at The Insider's involvement in global events that went beyond the forex market.

One email in particular caught Mark's attention. It contained a list of individuals, prominent figures in politics, finance, and technology, all marked as "partners." The Insider's influence seemed to extend far beyond currency manipulation.

"This is it," Mark whispered, his heart pounding. "We're on the verge of exposing The Insider's true identity and the extent of their plan."

David nodded, his eyes filled with determination. "We need to cross-reference this list with our contacts and gather more information. It's a delicate task, Mark. We can't afford to be discovered."

Mark agreed. They couldn't risk alerting The Insider's network prematurely. They needed to be meticulous, to gather evidence that would withstand scrutiny in a court of law.

As dawn broke, they continued their work, building a web of connections that would lead them closer to The Insider. But the more they uncovered, the darker and more dangerous the conspiracy appeared. It was a tangled web of power, deceit, and manipulation that reached the highest levels of influence.

Suddenly, a sharp knock at the cabin door interrupted their work. Mark's heart skipped a beat. They were supposed to be hidden, far away from anyone who might discover their location.

David reached for his concealed weapon as Mark cautiously approached the door. He peered through the peephole and saw a man in a dark suit standing outside, his face obscured by shadows.

Mark opened the door a crack, keeping his hand on his weapon. "Who are you, and how did you find us?"

The man in the dark suit didn't answer immediately. Instead, he handed Mark an envelope, his voice low and measured. "You're getting too close, Detective Turner. Consider this a warning."

Mark took the envelope, his heart sinking. Inside was a single photograph—a picture of his

daughter, Emily, playing in the park. The message was clear—back off or face the consequences.

David's voice was a tense whisper as he watched Mark's reaction. "Mark, we can't let them intimidate us. We're close to exposing The Insider. We need to push forward, for Emily and for justice."

Mark clenched his jaw, his determination unwavering. He knew they were in a perilous game, but he couldn't back down now. The pursuit of The Insider and the exposure of the currency conspiracy had become a matter of personal and global significance.

As Mark closed the cabin door, he knew that the shadows were closing in on them, that the web of deception and danger had tightened. But he also knew that they were closer than ever to uncovering the truth and stopping The Insider's plan from changing the world. The race against time had reached its most critical juncture, and Mark was prepared to face whatever challenges lay ahead.

The Unraveling

The days that followed were a tense blur of investigation and paranoia. Detective Mark Turner and David had returned to their covert safehouse in the woods, determined to press forward despite the ominous warning they had received. The photograph of Mark's daughter, Emily, served as a constant reminder of the stakes involved.

David had been working tirelessly to cross-reference the list of "partners" they had found on The Collector's encrypted server. Each name represented a potential link to The Insider and the conspiracy that threatened the world. Mark, on the other hand, had been in touch with his contacts within law enforcement, discreetly sharing their findings and requesting backup.

Late one night, David uncovered a significant lead. One of the names on the list, Jonathan Hollis, a prominent tech billionaire, had a history of suspicious financial transactions and political connections. It seemed that Hollis might be a key player in The Insider's network.

Mark leaned over David's shoulder as they examined the evidence. "Hollis could be the connection we've been searching for. If we can get close to him, we might get a lead on The Insider."

David nodded, his eyes filled with determination. "I've also found chatter on the dark web about a secret meeting that's scheduled to take place in the city. It could be where The Insider and their associates gather."

Mark's pulse quickened. This was their chance to confront The Insider directly, to unravel the conspiracy and expose the truth. "We need to infiltrate that meeting, David. It's our best shot at getting to the heart of this."

David's fingers flew across the keyboard as he accessed the details of the meeting. It was set to take place in an abandoned warehouse on the city's outskirts, a place known for its secrecy and security.

"We'll need a plan," Mark said, his mind racing. "We can't just walk in there. They'll be expecting trouble."

David leaned back in his chair, deep in thought. "We could pose as potential recruits. The Insider's network seems to be expanding, and they might be looking for new members."

Mark nodded in agreement. It was a risky strategy, but it was their best chance at gaining access to the meeting. "We'll need convincing cover stories and backgrounds. Let's get to work on our personas."

As they spent the following days crafting their new identities, Mark couldn't help but wonder about Emily's safety. The warning they had received had shaken him to the core, and he had taken every precaution to ensure her protection. She was staying with a trusted family friend, far away from the dangers that surrounded them.

Finally, the day of the secret meeting arrived. Mark and David dressed the part, adopting the personas of financial professionals seeking to join The Insider's operation. Their cover stories were carefully crafted, complete with fabricated backgrounds and references.

The abandoned warehouse loomed before them as they approached, its windows shattered and its exterior covered in graffiti. The air was thick with tension as they entered the dimly lit interior. The sound of hushed voices and footsteps echoed through the cavernous space.

Mark and David mingled with the other attendees, all of whom were masked and obscured in shadows. The atmosphere was suffused with secrecy and anticipation, and Mark couldn't help but feel like a small fish swimming in treacherous waters.

They waited for what felt like an eternity, their nerves on edge, until a figure stepped forward on a raised platform at the front of the warehouse. It was The Collector.

The Collector's voice was low and commanding as they addressed the assembled crowd. "Welcome, all. You have been chosen for your skills, your discretion, and your unwavering commitment to our cause. The time has come to reveal the next phase of The Insider's plan."

Mark and David exchanged a covert glance, their hearts pounding. This was their chance to gather vital information about The Insider's true identity and the extent of their plan.

The Collector continued, outlining a vision of global change and financial power that sent chills down Mark's spine. It was clear that The Insider's ambition extended far beyond the manipulation of currency markets; they sought to reshape the world order itself.

Then, as The Collector spoke of a final, decisive move that would set their plan into motion, Mark and David noticed something unusual. The masked attendees were divided into two groups—one group, including Mark and David, had been given white masks, while the others wore black masks.

"What does this mean?" David whispered, his voice barely audible over the murmurs of the crowd.

Mark's mind raced as he considered the implications. The division seemed significant, a signal of some sort, but its meaning remained unclear. They needed to gather more information.

As The Collector's speech continued, Mark noticed a masked figure in the black-masked group exchanging a subtle hand signal with another attendee. It was a signal Mark recognized—it was the same one used by the traders at the underground trading ring.

He leaned closer to David. "That's it, David. That's our lead. We need to follow that figure when this meeting ends."

David nodded in agreement, his eyes fixed on the figure in question. The Collector's speech was coming to a close, and the attendees began to disperse.

Mark and David subtly joined the black-masked group, blending in as best they could. They followed the figure who had given the signal, moving through the dimly lit corridors of the warehouse.

Finally, the figure entered a small room at the rear of the warehouse, and Mark and David discreetly followed. Inside, they found a set of computers and monitors, each displaying financial data and charts.

The figure removed their mask, revealing the face of a woman with a determined expression. Mark recognized her from the underground trading ring—the one who had issued the challenge. She was a key player in The Insider's network.

Before Mark and David could make a move, the woman spoke into a hidden microphone. "I've identified two new recruits who show promise. They've been following me."

Suddenly, the door to the room slammed shut, trapping Mark and David inside. They turned to see The Collector, their identity still concealed by a mask, standing in the doorway.

The Collector's voice was cold and menacing as they addressed Mark and David. "You two have proven yourselves resourceful, but your intrusion ends here. The Insider has eyes everywhere."

Mark's heart sank. They had walked right into a trap. The Insider's network was more formidable and well-connected than they had imagined.

The Collector gestured to the woman, who had taken a defensive stance. "Sarah, deal with them."

Sarah, the woman from the underground trading ring, approached, her eyes filled with determination. Mark and David were outnumbered and trapped, their escape routes cut off.

As Sarah moved closer, Mark couldn't help but wonder if this was the end of their pursuit, if The Insider's secrets would remain forever shrouded in darkness. But he also knew that giving up was not an option, not when so much was at stake.

As Sarah reached for a concealed weapon, Mark and David braced themselves for the inevitable confrontation, determined to fight for justice and to finally unravel the truth behind The Insider's conspiracy.

A Dangerous Gamble

In the dimly lit room of the abandoned warehouse, Detective Mark Turner and David stood trapped, cornered by Sarah, a key operative of The Insider's network. The Collector, still masked and ominous, watched their predicament with cold detachment, their voice laced with a chilling sense of authority.

"Sarah," The Collector instructed, "ensure they don't interfere with our plans any longer."

Sarah's eyes flickered with a mix of determination and reluctance as she moved closer to Mark and David, her weapon held at the ready. The room seemed to close in around them, the tension palpable.

Mark glanced at David, a silent exchange of resolve passing between them. They knew they were in a dire situation, but they had come too far to back down now. Their pursuit of justice and the exposure of The Insider's conspiracy demanded that they press forward.

With lightning speed, Sarah lunged forward, her weapon aimed at Mark. In that moment, Mark's training kicked in. He deftly disarmed Sarah, the weapon clattering to the floor. It was a tense standoff, and David had his own hands full grappling with another operative who had entered the room.

The Collector's masked face betrayed no emotion as they calmly observed the altercation. Mark and David's fight for survival had become a high-stakes game, one where every move could be their last.

Despite the odds stacked against them, Mark and David managed to subdue their adversaries. Sarah and the other operative lay incapacitated on the cold floor, their masks discarded.

Mark seized the opportunity to address The Collector, his voice determined. "Enough of this secrecy. It's time you reveal yourself, and we get the answers we've been seeking."

The Collector hesitated for a moment, their masked face betraying no emotion. Then, with deliberate slowness, they reached up and removed the mask, revealing a face that Mark had never seen before—a face that belonged to a woman in her forties with piercing green eyes and a demeanor that radiated authority.

"Detective Turner, you have proven to be quite resourceful," she said, her voice calm and measured. "You may call me Eleanor."

Mark's mind raced as he tried to make sense of the situation. Eleanor was not the person he had expected to find behind The Collector's mask. Her presence raised more questions than answers.

"Why have you been hiding in the shadows, Eleanor?" David demanded, his voice tinged with anger. "What is The Insider's true plan?"

Eleanor regarded them both with an air of superiority. "The Insider's plan is to create a new world order, one where the balance of power is shifted in our favor. But you're mistaken if you think you can stop it."

Mark couldn't help but feel a sense of foreboding at Eleanor's words. The

Insider's ambitions were more far-reaching and dangerous than he had ever imagined.

"We need to expose the truth, Eleanor," Mark insisted. "The world needs to know what you're planning."

Eleanor's expression remained resolute. "You have no idea what you're up against, Detective. The Insider's network is vast, and its influence extends far beyond what you can imagine."

Mark knew they were in a perilous situation. Eleanor was a formidable adversary, and The Insider's reach was more extensive than they had realized. They needed a plan, a way to turn the tables and uncover the full scope of the conspiracy.

David, his mind racing, spoke up. "Eleanor, we're willing to listen. Tell us your side of the story. Perhaps there's a way to prevent catastrophe without resorting to violence."

Eleanor regarded David with a hint of curiosity. "Very well. If you're willing to listen, then hear this: The Insider's plan is to dismantle the current global financial system, which they view as corrupt and unsustainable. They aim to create a new digital currency, one that transcends national borders and empowers individuals. They believe it will bring about a fairer, more just world."

Mark exchanged a skeptical glance with David. Eleanor's explanation sounded like a lofty ideal, but it raised more questions than answers. "And how do you plan to achieve this vision?"

Eleanor's gaze turned inward, as if contemplating her words carefully. "The details of The Insider's plan are known only to a select few, myself included. But I can assure you that it involves a complex series of events that will expose the weaknesses of the current system."

David pressed further, his voice unwavering. "What about the chaos and instability this plan will cause? Innocent people will suffer."

Eleanor's expression remained enigmatic. "Sometimes, change requires upheaval. The world has become complacent, entrenched in its flawed systems. The Insider's plan is a wake-up call, a catalyst for transformation."

Mark couldn't help but feel a sense of moral ambiguity in Eleanor's words. While the idea of challenging a corrupt financial system had its merits, the methods and consequences were deeply troubling.

"We can't condone a plan that causes harm to innocent lives," Mark said firmly. "Our duty is to protect the public and uphold the law."

Eleanor sighed, her gaze locking onto Mark's with an intensity that sent shivers down his spine. "You may have your ideals, Detective Turner, but the world is far more complex than black and white. The Insider's plan is in motion, and it cannot be stopped."

Before Mark could respond, a commotion outside the room caught their attention. The sound of approaching footsteps and raised voices signaled the arrival of reinforcements.

Eleanor's expression turned grim. "It seems our time here is at an end. We'll meet again, Detective Turner, but next time, you may not be so fortunate."

With that, Eleanor retreated, slipping away through a concealed exit just as a group of operatives burst into the room.

Mark and David knew they couldn't stay. They had narrowly escaped capture once, but they wouldn't be so lucky a second time. They fought their way past the operatives, making a daring escape through the labyrinthine corridors of the warehouse.

As they emerged into the night air, their breath visible in the cold, Mark couldn't help but feel a sense of frustration and urgency. The Insider's plan was in motion, and Eleanor remained an enigmatic and formidable adversary.

Their pursuit of justice had taken a dangerous turn, one

that led them deeper into the heart of a conspiracy that threatened to reshape the world. Mark knew they couldn't give up, not when the stakes were so high, and the need for the truth so paramount.

With determination in their hearts, Mark and David disappeared into the shadows, ready to continue their dangerous gamble in the pursuit of justice and the exposure of The Insider's conspiracy. The world was watching, and the final act of this high-stakes thriller was yet to unfold.

The Unveiling

The pursuit of The Insider and the exposure of their elaborate conspiracy had become a relentless race against time. Detective Mark Turner and David, his trusted ally and informant, had narrowly escaped The Insider's operatives in the abandoned warehouse. Now, they found themselves in the heart of the city, their minds filled with questions and determination.

Their encounter with Eleanor, the enigmatic figure behind The Collector's mask, had left them with a sense of urgency. The Insider's plan was in motion, and it was shrouded in secrecy. Mark and David knew they needed to act swiftly to prevent catastrophe.

Mark drove their inconspicuous sedan through the bustling streets, his gaze darting between the rearview mirror and the traffic ahead. They had managed to shake off their pursuers for now, but they couldn't afford to let their guard down.

"We need to find a way to expose The Insider's plan to the world," Mark said, his voice filled with resolve. "But we can't do it alone. We need help, and we need concrete evidence."

David nodded in agreement. "Eleanor mentioned that The Insider's plan involves exposing the weaknesses of the current financial system. We need to figure out what that means and how they intend to do it."

Their search for answers led them to a hidden network of contacts, individuals who had their own reasons for wanting to uncover The Insider's secrets. These contacts had been operating in the shadows, gathering information on The Insider's activities for years.

One such contact, a tech-savvy hacker named Alex, agreed to meet with Mark and David in a discreet location. They found themselves in a dimly lit underground bar, the air thick with secrecy and the low hum of conversation.

Alex, a wiry figure with a shock of unruly hair, greeted them with a nod. "You're the ones looking to expose The Insider?"

Mark and David exchanged a cautious glance before nodding. "That's right," Mark replied. "We need your help to uncover their plan and gather concrete evidence."

Alex leaned in closer, his voice barely above a whisper. "I've been tracking their digital footprint for a while. There have been unusual movements in the financial markets, and it all seems to lead back to The Insider's network."

Mark and David listened intently as Alex explained the intricacies of the digital trail he had been following. It was a complex web of transactions, hidden accounts, and encrypted messages that hinted at The Insider's influence in global financial events.

"Can you trace it back to a source?" David asked.

Alex nodded. "I've been working on it, and I believe I've pinpointed a key figure within their organization—a person known as 'The Orchestrator.' This individual seems to be coordinating the financial moves that will expose the system's vulnerabilities."

Mark felt a glimmer of hope. If they could identify The Orchestrator, it might lead them closer to The Insider's true identity and the heart of the conspiracy.

"What's our next move?" Mark inquired.

Alex leaned back, his eyes scanning the room for eavesdroppers. "I've set up a meeting with an insider who has ties to The Orchestrator. It's a risky move, but it's our best shot at getting more information."

David nodded, his expression determined. "We'll be there. When is the meeting?"

Alex handed them a small, encrypted device. "Tomorrow night, at a secure location. Use this to contact me. I'll provide you with the details and help you navigate the meeting."

As they left the underground bar, Mark and David knew that their gamble was far from over. They were one step closer to uncovering The Insider's secrets, but they were also walking deeper into the heart of danger.

The following night, they followed Alex's instructions to a hidden location on the outskirts of the city—a derelict industrial complex that had long been abandoned. The moon cast eerie shadows on the rusted structures, creating an atmosphere of tension and uncertainty.

Mark and David arrived at the designated meeting point, their senses heightened. They had no way of knowing what to expect, and the darkness seemed to close in around them.

Suddenly, a figure emerged from the shadows, their face obscured by a hood and a mask. It was their contact, the insider with ties to The Orchestrator.

The insider's voice was disguised, a deliberate measure to protect their identity. "You're here for information on The Orchestrator, correct?"

Mark and David exchanged a wary glance before nodding. "That's right. We need to expose The Insider's plan."

The insider stepped closer, their movements cautious. "The Orchestrator is a high-ranking member of The Insider's network. They are the mastermind behind the financial moves that will destabilize the current system."

Mark leaned in, his voice low. "Do you have any information on The Orchestrator's identity or whereabouts?"

The insider hesitated before replying, "I can provide you with a lead, but it won't be easy to follow. The Orchestrator is elusive, and their true identity is known only to a few."

David pressed further. "We need something concrete. A name, a location—anything that can help us track them down."

The insider leaned closer, their voice a mere whisper. "There have been rumors of a secret meeting. It's where The Orchestrator is known to communicate with other high-ranking members of The Insider's network. It's called 'The Convergence,' and it's happening soon."

Mark's heart raced. "Tell us more about this meeting. When and where?"

The insider handed them a small, encrypted device, similar to the one Alex had provided. "This will give you access to The Convergence. It's a heavily guarded event, but with this, you should be able to infiltrate and gather the information you seek."

As Mark and David left the meeting, their heads filled with new leads and a sense of urgency, they couldn't help but feel that they were closing in on The

Insider's true identity and the heart of the conspiracy. The Convergence was their next target—a high-stakes gamble that could either bring them closer to the truth or plunge them deeper into the shadows.

The night was dark and cold as they made their way back to their safehouse. They knew that every move they made was a risk, but they were driven by a determination to expose The Insider's plan and to prevent the chaos it threatened to unleash upon the world.

As they entered the safehouse, Mark's thoughts turned to Emily, his daughter, and the danger that had encroached upon their lives. The warning they had received, the threats, and the relentless pursuit had taken a toll on their sense of security.

But Mark also knew that they couldn't back down now, not when the world was on the brink of upheaval. The final act of this high-stakes thriller was yet to unfold, and Mark and David were prepared to stake everything in their pursuit of justice and the exposure of The Insider's conspiracy.

With the encrypted device in their possession, they were one step closer to unraveling the secrets that had remained hidden for far too long. The unveiling of The Insider's plan was within reach, and the world was watching, waiting for the truth to emerge.

Infiltration

The Convergence was the linchpin in The Insider's intricate plan—a clandestine gathering of high-ranking members where the final details of their scheme would be revealed. Detective Mark Turner and David had obtained the encrypted device that would give them access to this elusive meeting. It was a high-stakes gamble, one that could expose The Insider's true identity and intentions or plunge them further into the shadows.

Mark and David had spent hours studying the information provided by their contact, the insider with ties to The Orchestrator. The Convergence was set to take place in an abandoned, heavily guarded facility on the outskirts of the city. It was a place where secrets were traded, and power shifted in the blink of an eye.

The night of the meeting had arrived, and the two men found themselves parked in a nondescript van, cloaked in the darkness of a nearby alley. The encrypted device, their key to infiltrating The Convergence, rested in David's hands.

Mark's voice was filled with a mix of determination and unease. "Once we're inside, we need to stay inconspicuous, blend in with the attendees. The last thing we want is to draw attention to ourselves."

David nodded, his fingers poised over the device. "Agreed. We'll play our parts and gather as much information as we can. We need concrete evidence of The Insider's identity and their plan."

With a final glance at the digital readout on the device, David initiated the sequence. A hidden message appeared, providing them with the location of The Convergence and a series of instructions on how to gain entry.

The abandoned facility loomed before them—a fortress of shadows and secrets. Armed guards patrolled the perimeter, their movements precise and unwavering. The sense of danger hung in the air, a palpable tension that seemed to grow with each passing moment.

Mark and David followed the instructions carefully, slipping past the guards unnoticed. They entered the facility through a concealed entrance, their senses on high alert. The heart of The Insider's operation awaited them, a place where the future of the financial world was being decided.

As they moved deeper into the facility, they found themselves in a vast, dimly lit chamber. Rows of masked attendees were seated in a circular arrangement, their faces obscured, their identities concealed. The air was heavy with anticipation.

In the center of the chamber, a raised platform stood, bathed in a soft, eerie light. It was here that The Orchestrator, the elusive figure behind The Insider's financial moves, was rumored to appear.

Mark and David took their seats among the attendees, careful not to draw attention to themselves. They wore masks, their identities hidden, and listened as the murmurs of conversation filled the chamber. The secrecy and tension were palpable, a testament to the power and influence of The Insider's network.

Minutes turned into hours as Mark and David waited for The Orchestrator's appearance. The anticipation weighed on them, and they couldn't help but wonder if they were walking into a trap, if The Insider had somehow become aware of their presence.

Finally, the room fell silent as a figure stepped onto the raised platform. It was The Orchestrator, their identity still shrouded in shadows. Their voice was low and commanding as they addressed the assembled attendees.

"Welcome, members of The Insider's network. The time has come to unveil the final phase of our plan—a plan that will expose the weaknesses of the current financial system and pave the way for a new world order."

Mark and David exchanged a covert glance. This was their moment, their chance to gather vital information about The Orchestrator and the true extent of The Insider's conspiracy.

The Orchestrator continued, outlining a series of meticulously coordinated financial moves that would send shockwaves through the global markets. It was a plan designed to exploit vulnerabilities, to disrupt the status quo, and to bring about a radical shift in power.

As Mark and David listened, they couldn't help but feel a sense of dread. The Insider's vision was one of chaos and upheaval, and innocent lives would be caught in the crossfire.

But amid the intricate details of The Insider's plan, one thing became clear—the identity of The Orchestrator remained hidden, and their true intentions remained elusive.

"We need a name, a face," Mark whispered to David. "We can't leave here without that information."

David nodded, his eyes fixed on The Orchestrator. "We'll have to act quickly. When they step down from the platform, we'll follow them."

As The Orchestrator's speech drew to a close, Mark and David readied themselves for the next phase of their dangerous gamble. The attendees began to disperse, their conversations hushed and guarded.

Finally, The Orchestrator descended from the platform and moved toward a concealed exit. Mark and David followed discreetly, their hearts pounding. They knew that this was their only chance to uncover The Orchestrator's true identity.

As they stepped into a dimly lit corridor, Mark and David moved closer to The Orchestrator, their footsteps echoing softly. The figure remained shrouded in shadows, their pace measured and deliberate.

Then, just as Mark and David were closing in, The Orchestrator turned a corner, disappearing from view. Mark and David quickened their pace, their adrenaline surging.

But when they reached the corner, The Orchestrator was gone. They had vanished into thin air, leaving no trace behind.

Mark's heart sank as he realized that they had come so close, only to lose their quarry. It was a bitter disappointment, and it left them with more questions than answers.

David's voice was tinged with frustration. "We can't let them slip away. We need to find another way to uncover The Orchestrator's identity."

Mark nodded in agreement. They had risked everything to infiltrate The Convergence, and they couldn't afford to leave empty-handed. The pursuit of justice and the exposure of The Insider's conspiracy demanded that they press forward.

With determination in their hearts, Mark and David retreated into the shadows, ready to regroup and continue their relentless pursuit. The unveiling of The Insider's secrets was within reach, and they were determined to uncover the truth, no matter the cost. The world was watching, and the final act of this high-stakes thriller was yet to unfold.

A Dangerous Revelation

The pursuit of The Insider and the exposure of their elaborate conspiracy had brought Detective Mark Turner and David to the brink of revelation. They had infiltrated The Convergence, a clandestine meeting of high-ranking members, in a daring gamble to uncover The Insider's true identity and intentions. But as The Orchestrator, the enigmatic figure behind The Insider's financial moves, had eluded their grasp, they found themselves faced with the daunting task of finding another way to expose the truth.

Mark and David retreated from the abandoned facility, their senses on high alert. They had narrowly escaped capture, and the sense of danger still clung to them like a shadow. The night air was cold and unforgiving, a stark contrast to the heated tension of The Convergence.

"We were so close," David muttered, frustration evident in his voice. "The Orchestrator slipped through our fingers."

Mark's jaw clenched as he wrestled with his own disappointment. "But we can't give up now. We have leads, contacts within The Insider's network. We'll find another way to uncover the truth."

Their first course of action was to regroup with Alex, the tech-savvy hacker who had been tracking The Insider's digital footprint. They arranged to meet in a secluded location, away from prying eyes and electronic surveillance.

The meeting took place in a dimly lit underground hideout. Alex, the wiry hacker with unruly hair, greeted them with a mix of determination and caution.

"Getting into The Convergence was a major achievement," Alex acknowledged, "but we need to keep the momentum going. I've been digging deeper into The Orchestrator's digital trail. It's a complex web, but I'm making progress."

Mark leaned forward, his expression intent. "Any leads on The Orchestrator's true identity?"

Alex hesitated before replying, "Not yet. But I've uncovered a series of encrypted communications between The Orchestrator and another high-ranking member of The Insider's network. They use code names—'The Architect' and 'The Enforcer.'"

David furrowed his brow. "We need to identify these individuals. They could be the key to unraveling The Insider's conspiracy."

Alex nodded in agreement. "I've been working on tracing their digital footprints. It's a delicate process, and I'm using every resource available. But we need something more concrete."

Mark's mind raced as he considered their options. They had come too far to back down now, and The Insider's true intentions remained a dangerous enigma.

"Keep working on it, Alex," Mark said firmly. "We'll need any information you can find on 'The Architect' and 'The Enforcer.' They may hold the key to exposing The Insider."

Their next lead came from an unexpected source—a disgruntled member of The Insider's network who had grown disillusioned with their radical plan. The insider, who went by the code name 'The Dissenter,' reached out to Mark and David in secret, offering to provide crucial information in exchange for protection and immunity.

They arranged a clandestine meeting in a deserted warehouse on the outskirts of the city. Mark and David arrived, their senses on high alert. The air was thick with tension as they awaited The Dissenter's arrival.

Finally, a figure emerged from the shadows, their face obscured by a hood and a mask. It was The Dissenter, their voice a mixture of fear and determination.

"I've seen enough," The Dissenter began, "The Insider's plan is not what it seems. They're not interested in creating a fairer world. They're interested in power and control."

Mark exchanged a glance with David. This was the break they had been waiting for—an insider willing to reveal The Insider's true intentions.

The Dissenter continued, "The Architect and The Enforcer are the key players in The Insider's network. They hold the knowledge and resources to expose the plan's real purpose."

Mark leaned in closer, his voice low. "Can you provide us with any information on their identities or whereabouts?"

The Dissenter hesitated before replying, "I can give you a location where you might find The Architect. But it's heavily guarded, and you'll need to move quickly."

David pressed further. "Tell us everything you know, every detail that can help us."

A DANGEROUS REVELATION

The Dissenter provided a location—a hidden facility on the outskirts of the city where The Architect was known to operate. It was a risky move, but it was their best chance at finding the elusive figure who might hold the key to The Insider's true identity and plan.

Mark and David left the meeting with a renewed sense of purpose. They had uncovered a potential lead that could bring them closer to unraveling The Insider's secrets. The Architect and The Enforcer were names that had eluded them for too long, and it was time to shine a light on the darkness.

The following night, Mark and David, cloaked in darkness and determination, arrived at the hidden facility. Armed guards patrolled the perimeter, their presence a stark reminder of the danger that surrounded them.

They moved with precision, stealthily navigating the facility's intricate layout. The air was thick with tension as they drew closer to their objective—the location where The Architect was rumored to operate.

Finally, they reached a sealed door, guarded by armed personnel. Mark and David exchanged a silent nod, their heartbeats echoing in their ears. With a burst of adrenaline, they breached the door, their weapons at the ready.

Inside, they found a room bathed in dim light, rows of computer monitors and servers lining the walls. At the center of the room, a figure worked diligently at a console, their back turned to the intruders.

It was The Architect, their identity still concealed. They were unaware of Mark and David's presence, focused on their task. This was the moment they had been waiting for—the chance to uncover The Architect's true identity and expose The Insider's plan.

With careful steps, Mark and David moved closer to The Architect, their hearts pounding in their chests. They had come too far to back down now, and the fate of the world hung in the balance.

But as they reached the figure and moved to reveal their identity, The Architect turned, their face obscured by a mask. It was the same mask worn by The Collector and The Orchestrator—a symbol of The Insider's secrecy and power.

Mark's voice was filled with frustration and determination. "Remove the mask. We need to see your face."

The Architect remained unmoved, their posture unwavering. "You may have come this far, but you will not reveal my identity. The Insider's plan is in motion, and it cannot be stopped."

David's voice was tinged with anger. "We know the truth about The Insider. We know their plan is not about creating a fairer world, but about power and control."

The Architect's response was enigmatic. "The world is a complex place, Detective Turner. Sometimes, drastic measures are necessary to bring about change."

Mark couldn't help but feel a sense of moral ambiguity in The Architect's words. While the idea of challenging a corrupt system had its merits, the methods and consequences were deeply troubling.

"We can't let you continue down this path," Mark said firmly. "The Insider's secrets must be exposed."

With a sudden, fluid motion, The Architect activated a concealed device, triggering alarms throughout the facility. Armed guards stormed into the room, their weapons trained on Mark and David.

It was a perilous standoff, a dangerous revelation that had turned the tide against them. Mark and David knew they were in a dire situation, trapped by The Insider's network and their unwavering resolve to protect their secrets.

As the guards closed in, Mark and David exchanged a determined glance. They had come too far to turn back now, and the pursuit of justice demanded that they press forward.

With a defiant resolve, they made a daring escape, engaging in a fierce firefight as they fought their way through the facility's labyrinthine corridors. Bullets flew, and the stakes were higher than ever.

The world was on the brink of upheaval, and Mark and David were determined to prevent catastrophe. The Insider's plan was in motion, but the final act of this high-stakes thriller had yet to unfold. The danger was relentless, but their pursuit of justice remained unwavering, and the truth was within reach, waiting to be unveiled.

www.ingramcontent.com/pod-product-compliance
Lightning Source LLC
LaVergne TN
LVHW050027080526
838202LV00069B/6940